SONG OF STARS

ELISE

Song Of Stars

Elise

ELISE

Song of stars

Copyright © 2021 Elise
All rights reserved.
No part of this book may be reproduced or used in
any manner without written permission of the
copyright owner except for the use of quotations in a
book review.

ELISE

Also by ELISE

STORIES ON HER LIPS

ELISE

Song of stars

The beauty of a song is that you're sharing the music inside you. The lyrics are poetry and the melody is a language we can all feel.

Music has always been a lifeline to connect to others in a deeper and magical way.

We listen to songs, and we sing them, we always will.

Songs that tell stories, songs that engrave a moment forever in our hearts, songs that capture a feeling.

As we sing to the beat of our hearts, we can hear the stars singing with us.

These poems are songs in their own way and when I write them, I hear the music in my mind.

So sing your song, and you'll hear the song of stars.

ELISE

Song of stars

For the ones who sing their song…

ELISE

And for the stars who sing with us…

ELISE

Song of stars

Poetry, Prose, Songs

ELISE

Song of stars

I breathed in the smoke from the turquoise fire
and turned my bloodshot eyes to the deep blue sky
her glistening embers thrumming in answer
to my own thundering heart
'come on, let's go sing with the stars'

ELISE

Song of stars

It's like the thoughts in my head
painted a clearer picture of life
under a canvas of pure starlight

ELISE

Song of stars

        I woke from the fever dream
            my heart pulsing
          with the beat of stars

ELISE

Song of stars

In midnight's lost breath
I have found myself haunted
by songs and stories and stars

ELISE

Song of stars

    And when the clock strikes thirteen
          and all worldly dust
      fades away into nothingness
    I'll hear the beating of my heart
       singing the song of stars

ELISE

Song of stars

We know the lyrics that can't be taught
lightning dances in our thoughts
this revolution walks with war
guard the key to your mind's door
at last, I know the voice inside my head
hello old friend, it's true what you said

ELISE

Song of stars

A song of ancient promises
sang into the flames tonight
a melody rises and flies on broken arrows
all I've ever known
sealed with a kiss of fire

ELISE

Song of stars

> Your ambient magic sings
> with midnight's music
> and explodes in bursts
> of deep indigo, black velvet and burning gold

ELISE

Song of stars

> Violet fox
> jumping between constellations
> his tale blazing with amber fire
> as he paints the darkness
> in between his stars

ELISE

Song of stars

She told her story in the inky depths
of midnight's waters
each word sending
gentle ripples into the deep
her voice like silk
on the shimmering surface
paintings that come alive
on wings of starlight
I could have sworn I heard
a single tear trickle down her face
and in that moment,
I saw a star fall from above
all the way down
and maybe for no other reason
than something ancient and alive
stirring inside me that night
I felt the pull to be with her
in her story
and so, I let my tears
sparkle with the night

ELISE

Song of stars

Rebels rumbling in Venice's sunken secrets
she found treasure in her own heart
and carried it to the shores of forbidden maps
meet me where it all began

ELISE

Song of stars

She walks on forgotten tracks of ash and bone
and blows kisses of embers
into the mist's mouth
on and on the trail burns
lighting hidden ways for wanderers

ELISE

Song of stars

> I felt the sweetness
> in the surrender of your heart to me
> and saw the glow in your veins
> as we ventured on this journey
> lost in your lilac eyes
> taste of your love makes me feel so alive

ELISE

Song of stars

Gold, turquoise and emerald lights
chased all the sparkles in the ebony sky
her unconquerable spirit soars so far
and she's singing her song of stars

ELISE

Song of stars

She sipped the nectar laced wine
but it was like she was pouring all her dreams into the cup
and she heard a voice whisper
'in the sky there's a story of stars
and beating loud, is the song in your heart'

ELISE

Song of stars

Sunset of emerald songs and golden hearts
melody of courage in her soul
and she smiles to the world
'here I am'

ELISE

Song of stars

Midnight masquerade
show me who you really are
I know the game
but I want to see your heart

ELISE

Song of stars

You played your song on that grand piano with candlelight
and I walked across the marble floor
all the way to the light in your mind
and you thought of how you might play me instead
and we both knew your favourite way to get the music from inside me

ELISE

Song of stars

> I'm a dreamer in a world of nightmares
> forever and always a lost girl

ELISE

Song of stars

The lure of your darkness
made me want to dance
in the shadows with you
and forget the torments of
all the ages I've spent without you

ELISE

Song of stars

> Victory tasted of fire and honey
> but no trumpets roared
> or horns with wings
> no sound but our hearts
> beating to the song of stars

ELISE

Song of stars

> She carried a wooden lantern with an orange flame
> that danced with the yellow stars on her blue gown
> and as she peered through the glass
> the sugared snow swept like dust around her face
> and she knew a storm was brewing in the cauldron
> and she was the one with the lightning

ELISE

Song of stars

> I felt her glorious passion shower over me
> as she twirled her body inside the dark sky
> adorned with pulsing stars
> she revelled in her feminine magic
> endless delight pouring in her eyes

ELISE

Song of stars

> Alone in the mountains
> the glistening snow in starlight
> like a dream I had dreamt long ago
> it's so silent
> I can hear the whistles of the world
> whispering stories of stars and dreams

ELISE

Song of stars

A train journey through purple peaks and deep ravines
take me anywhere on this road
my eyes will shine with hope
it's more than what it seems
farewell, here I go

ELISE

Song of stars

In the fire I saw a wolf made of flames
wanting to fly with the eagle above
your magic is different but the same
he can soar but you can run

ELISE

Song of stars

Always live in a way that fuels your fire

ELISE

Song of stars

These ruins are full of ghosts
voices echoing in the stone
a memory of a dream
how could I not believe

ELISE

Song of stars

In this story,
when you sing your song to the stars
the stars sing theirs back to you

ELISE

Electrified with the memories
of your love
tonight it's all or nothing
so let's dance to forget
and sing to remember
oh baby, it's not over yet

ELISE

Song of stars

In one moment,
I decided to pour the water of words
from my drowning heart
and once the stars began falling
I knew I couldn't stop them
and I didn't want to

ELISE

Song of stars

Stormy nights in the ocean's heart
sailing toward that North Star
smell of salt and sweet dreams
tonight I remember what it all means

ELISE

Song of stars

Once you hear the faint thrumming of the song inside
you create your own paradise
it's the music inside your mind
playing to your beat, always on time

ELISE

Song of stars

        I watched you thinking about the thoughts in my pretty head
                but trust me, they aren't pretty thoughts

ELISE

Song of stars

When desert kings sing of tales told
and wild horses run where the sun kisses the sky
songs sewn with threads of gold
oh my love, on destiny's wings, we'll ride

ELISE

Song of stars

You will never fully understand me
I'll forever be a star-studded mystery

ELISE

Song of stars

Silhouettes of you in a cluster of stars
your memories alive in my heart
will you ever come back to me in this world?
when I'm with you I remember the girl
who would ride with the stars until she bled
I want to feel like that vivacious dreamer again

ELISE

Song of stars

In this teenage wasteland
we all know but few understand
broken dreams of youth run hand in hand
with those not afraid to take a stand

ELISE

Song of stars

It's like greeting an old friend
I once knew inside a dream
finding again that unbreakable thread
and following it to your soul's starry stream

ELISE

Song of stars

A poet's heart beats true
a dreamers soul sings to you
and in your eyes, a story told
words worth more than gold

ELISE

Song of stars

> Maybe it was the venom from your bite
> that made me hallucinate
> but I swear I saw you in the golden sky
> wink at me and scream 'we'll never die'

ELISE

Song of stars

She inhaled the misty air
then exhaled a shape of a wolf in the smoke
running wild and dangerous
'you see, I'm a wolf inside, fierce and untameable'

ELISE

Song of stars

Strange things happened on the night she came back
it's like the trees started to breathe again
and nature's heart began to sing

ELISE

Song of stars

I'll keep my ace of hearts close to my chest
you were always the Jack of Jokers I loved best

ELISE

Song of stars

Enveloped in the purple sky
ebony smoke rising high
and I spoke with my tears
telling secrets to midnight's ears

ELISE

Song of stars

Emerald embers call out my name
stronger pulse but the same
no more holding back, there's no time left now
I know what I want, and I know how

ELISE

Song of stars

It seemed all the lights were on tonight
orange wax candles and shooting stars
glowing sparks healing my heart
power of a touch in lovers' delight

ELISE

Song of stars

To go on through the treacherous jungle of noises and nightmares
to bandage your bruised heart
to remain unbowed to heavy expectations
and to still sing your own song in a world of remixes and covers
I promise you; you'll get to where you're meant to be

ELISE

Song of stars

Sprinkle me in velvet kisses
tell me tales of your travels
along the sandy roads
of forgotten dreams
there's nothing that tastes sweeter
than a story lived whole-heartedly

ELISE

In this game of words
choose yours as wisely
as you'd choose the person you'd share them with
they'll be with you always

ELISE

Song of stars

Black boots click on old streets
of cobblestones in the crisp winter's bite
steam of my breath spirals in the air
toward hidden clouds
like dusty smoke from a wild horse
with hooves of steel
as she gallops into the mist

ELISE

Song of stars

She breathed in the night's aromatic breeze
and blew stardust from her lungs with a smile he'd never seen before
'oh, there's something sparkling in the air tonight'

ELISE

Song of stars

Yellow lanterns light the way
when day is night and night is day
all you know and feel and see
is a song, a secret and a mystery

ELISE

Song of stars

Her song is a mystery even to herself
deep into her mind she delves
perhaps she'll find the truth in a story
and scrolls that tell of times of glory
she'll sing with her music under the stars
and dream of the mystery in her heart

ELISE

Song of stars

A storm of stars gathers speed in her mind
her electric thoughts run wild
how intimate the conversations inside your head
the words you say only to yourself

Song of stars

> I've found no cure for curiosity
> because your mind is meant to seek

ELISE

Song of stars

If you ever need me
look to the starry sky
and when I see your eyes
and you see mine
there I'll be

ELISE

Song of stars

>Water gardens with lotus flowers
>open my petals, feel my showers
>I'll bloom whatever the weather
>I have the sweetest, invigorating nectar

ELISE

Song of stars

You were my nightlight
in the vast darkness across the ages
each time your goodbye cut me deep
and engraved a memory in my heart
the night became my reverie
where I'd dream of our midnight meetings

ELISE

Song of stars

> You and me,
> we bleed the same stars

ELISE

Song of stars

> Painting stars on her skin
> a story of phantoms begins
> make it real tonight my dear
> songs reach many ears
> I know you've got the power for what it takes
> you can do anything, you'll never break

ELISE

Song of stars

It's like my imagination dances with the ether
and we're both moving to the same music

ELISE

Song of stars

I gazed into those icy blue and white flames
water and snow mingling their magic
in the ebony cauldron
and I saw winter's silky fox at the edge of the world
watching the turquoise lights dance in the sky
and I was gazing at that mischievous twinkle in his eyes

ELISE

Song of stars

I'll be midnight's mistress for eternity
he's always felt like a reflection of my soul

ELISE

Song of stars

Live in life's wonderland
unlocking its secrets
and living its joys

ELISE

Song of stars

> How could I ever forget the stories
> that the voice inside my head tells me?

ELISE

Song of stars

I've always dreamed of running with the wild wolf inside me
that so many have tried to cage
to run with a heart on fire
under those never-fading stars

ELISE

Song of stars

The inky pool of swirling stars
and hollow dreams
of blood from vows made
and honey from lips
of destiny in hearts
and doom in night's gaze
oh my friend, it's all a game

ELISE

Song of stars

Her thoughts were laced with the end game of rebellion
and deep in the witching hour
many other thoughts gathered with the strength
of all the rebels with dreams keeping them awake
deep in that magic hour

ELISE

Song of stars

The constellations in her eyes
were more beautiful to look at
than the ones in the sky

ELISE

Song of stars

It began with her song
the night she promised
all the stars in her sky
she would not let her spirit be broken
for they could never destroy her soul

ELISE

Song of stars

>Maybe we choose when to hear the music
>or maybe it chooses us

ELISE

Song of stars

After everything you've been through
don't you dare become like the rest of them

ELISE

Song of stars

Staying awake long into the midnight hours is like
waiting to greet an old friend
who only appears in your dreams

ELISE

Song of stars

That night,
I'm sure the stars toasted to our love
with honey dipped dreams
and soul food

ELISE

Song of stars

In midnight's mayhem
when the stars begin to sing
and the sky's heart opens
I'll be on the hill by the river
dreaming and awake all at once
whispering the song of stars

ELISE

Written Legend

So it's come to this, I knew it would
I feel the fire in my blood
That spark of life we have inside
The greatest battles are in our minds
You were like a moth to the flame
Until the flame you became
Maybe I wrote it long ago
What I feel is all I know

Whispers in the wild night
You hit home with a lightning strike
Just keep wandering along the road
You'll get to where you need to go
We're the dreamers in the stories you were told
Our blood runs true with burning gold

I've got some stories in my heart
Beating loud, my North star
You tell me your story and I'll tell you mine
And we'll meet at midnight before the chime
And cheers to life with legends and wine

I hear my voice echoing back to me
Sounds like a never-ending story
In these dreams of mine, I'm free
It's a legend written, it's meant to be
Call it fate, it was destined
Our story, a written legend

ELISE

Song of stars

It was the look of desire in your eyes
before we kissed under stormy skies
I'll still write this dream knowing what's at stake
with you I'm dreaming when I'm awake

It's a dream I wrote for you
with ink and stars of gold and blue
a promise buried deep within the mist
bound with blood and my kiss

ELISE

Song of stars

We're the ones that haunt your dreams
our strength doesn't weaken when we bleed
you've got the rebel's fire in you
stop denying
start flying
the rebel youth is you

ELISE

Song of stars

Secrets in my head
I see stars, the story starts again
A kiss of life tonight
My breath hits and I strike
Kiss my lips, my heart, my soul
Who was I long ago?

ELISE

Song of stars

Twilight's cloak of stars and memories wrapped around my body
as I tiptoed on the clouds
and blew golden dust
onto the dreamers and the stargazers

ELISE

Turquoise Fire

A colour of sea, sky and soul
Luminescent in nature, her fiery glow
Beauty in those who run wild on their own
We don't need permission, this is our show
The ones not afraid to play their own song
Dancers and dreamers will burn on and on

This is a story I've heard before
A legend whispered where rebels soar
Do you recognise the sound of your heart?
The light in your eyes is the spark

Write your story in those turquoise flames
Your paradise fire burns untamed

I've got that turquoise fire in my veins
Stars glow one and the same
I burn with a different sound
Song of stars sings lost and found
I'm flying with eternal desire
Heart singing with that turquoise fire

ELISE

Taste Of My Tears

The deepest cuts are the ones you make yourself
How can I begin to breathe again?
I betrayed my heart
Now I feel a permanent scar
I want to forgive myself, but I don't know how
Nothing in this world can bring me back now

I played the villain for a chapter
Tell me now what comes after
I still feel that bitter, unbearable pain
Memories I'd sooner forget, fill my mind again
Near the abyss, all alone
Still a flicker of hope lingers on

I've got to own everything I've done
Drive out the doubt, fill me with love
I am my own darkness, I am my own light
My tears are wings, watch me fly
It's not over, it's still my fight
The hurt just means I'm alive

In my mouth is the taste of tears and blood
My secrets safe on my tongue
I'll drown in my tears before I go to the slaughter
I'll survive like always; I can breathe underwater

ELISE

Song of stars

Tell me a story so I can sleep at night
The story of the stars in your eyes
I know your magic is true
You've got the real in you
Lost girls dancing where fairies sing
This is just the beginning

Your tales have not been forgotten
Lost in a daydream, your cosmic imagination
When I don't know what's real and true
In a heartbeat I turn to you

Your infinite magic I inhale
When nothing is certain, I know you're the real fairy-tale

ELISE

Song of stars

Signals of torches under cloudy skies
no one can stop you
when you've got the fire in your eyes

ELISE

Song of stars

> Dancing with the darkness
> is only dancing with
> the hidden parts of yourself

ELISE

Song of stars

'Because when it's my heart on the line
I know what is mine'
and she smiled with utter confidence and wit
she was the epitome of a woman
in love with her stars
'Oh darling, no one tells stories like I do'

ELISE

Song of stars

> The melody of her night is alive
> and playing in the shadow of your eyes

Song of stars

Another breath
her voice sings true
forget the rest
it's only you
and the fireflies came out to play
and it all goes away
just that moment with the stars in her mind
singing with the darkness and the light
and all she knew was the music inside her
magic of her song rising higher
one more breath as the words leave her tongue
on that note she'll always be young
and her breath flowed through her like a flame
eternal and wondrous, her beauty will always remain
and she let it move her in a dance with her song
the feeling of pure euphoria in her heart will always belong

ELISE

Song of stars

Once upon a timeless age, I did care
but I fought on my own, you weren't there
now it's just me, my burden to bear

ELISE

Song of stars

I write words onto paper, and it sings
stories spread with ink-soaked wings

ELISE

Song of stars

With the music of the stars
we'll party near and far
swing Orion's belt around my hips
sing with our song on my lips
drunk on desire and foxberries
we dance and make this night legendary

ELISE

Song of stars

He knew the words to say
that sent electric pulses of passion in my veins
time had no voice when he was near
the only one to know the colour of my tears
we lived by the beat of our hearts
always together and always apart

ELISE

Song of stars

Strip it down to your essence
show me your soul
who are you really?

ELISE

Song of stars

I was alone, sitting at the glass bottle bar
the amethyst colours catching the light from the setting sun
birds chirping as they fluttered to the fountains for a drink of comfort
the city began to come alive with the noise of people's wasted dreams
and he asked what flavour poison I'd be drinking
I mustered a smile but barely hid my sorrow
'fill my cup with your hopes and dreams
and I'll drink to your voyage forevermore'

ELISE

Song of stars

A stolen kiss embroidered in her midnight dress
as the stars caress her snowy hair
that billows past her hips like a snowfall
a white wolf as she roams the forest
every night in search for a story, to ease the hunger in her heart

ELISE

Song of stars

A song is a love letter
you write to yourself
when you need to hear
the music of your soul

ELISE

Song of stars

She told a myth of stars in the voice of midnight
like she was there when the legend was written
she made it real, if only for this night

ELISE

Song of stars

She always seemed more beautiful
when she was writing stories
because she didn't have to pretend
to be anyone else

ELISE

Song of stars

> Writing stories
> feels like healing
> the wounds with
> golden dust
> in my blood

ELISE

Song of stars

All through the ages
we have gathered in great halls
and beside humble hearths
to hear stories from the lips
of those brave enough
to dare to live

ELISE

Song of stars

We'd both seen the dripping darkness
in each other's hearts
and we'd loved each other
because we knew
the courage it took to reveal
those deep, hidden parts of our souls
to another person
when we could barely
look at them ourselves

ELISE

Song of stars

They recognised each other
by the same gold face paint they wore
but they remembered each other
by the music from their souls

ELISE

Song of stars

Oh, how you dance with all the colours of your soul
I can't wait to see the art you create

ELISE

Song of stars

I journeyed all through the cold night's embrace
and I'll never forget the first sip of mulberry tea
herbal healing to lift the spirits effortlessly
and on I went again without a trace

ELISE

Song of stars

> She fiercely protected her mind
> from the slow decay of normality
> she was crazy, she knew it and she loved it

ELISE

He would always catch her
playing with her golden necklace
as she stared into the distance
at something that wasn't there

Song of stars

Once she heard the thrum of that electric music
everything was lost in the sound
lost from time and reality
dreaming in this fantasy
as her body moved with every spark
of electricity in her veins

ELISE

Song of stars

She gazed into the depths of his black heart
and saw a fortress of swirling nightmares and secrets

ELISE

Song of stars

Her song is written in the stars
and every once in the midnight hour
it pours down onto him
and the fireworks in her eyes
are the only sign that she was even here

ELISE

Song of stars

She owns every spark of flame in her heart

ELISE

Song of stars

And at last
she let it all back in
and it hit home like
a bolt of lightning
it was always up to her
whether it stopped her heart
or made it start again

ELISE

Song of stars

"I took her to my favourite place to drink the darkest wine
and escape in the sweet smell of vanilla incense
and I couldn't help but feel
she'd walked many lives
and had a mind of unparalleled wisdom,
but a body ripe and prime
for a night of lovemaking, passion drenching antics."

-Old soul, young heart

ELISE

Song of stars

> Maybe it's the stories we tell ourselves
> that are the wisest of friends

ELISE

Song of stars

Yellow lights in your soul
dancing with the blue lights of mine
and what beautiful fireworks we created
in the darkness of the shadow of the world

ELISE

Song of stars

> We danced and drank and dived
> into the infinite moment
> of forgetting the thoughts
> inside our heads

ELISE

Song of stars

All fireworks leave a trace of smoke behind
you either wait for it to pass
or you learn how to breathe the air
as you walk through it

ELISE

Song of stars

> I've got my heart of courage on tonight
> and the diamonds in my eyes
> a dress of silver and gold
> as we put on a show
> toasting to lives of risk and romance
> vibrant echoes of this lifelong dance

ELISE

Song of stars

Every night in my dreams
I meet the voice inside my head

ELISE

Song of stars

> Song lyrics remember when you sang them
> just as you remember the melody they belong to

ELISE

Song of stars

You're only here inside my mind
if it's all a dream, are you still alive?

ELISE

Song of stars

You gave me a love bite on my skin
when I wanted you to kiss my soul

ELISE

Song of stars

Lost in the song of ink and stars
dust from the notes in my heart
feel the music of a spark
dancing with the sound of the dark

Song of stars

Cut me open and fill me up
with all the music
spilling out of your soul

ELISE

Song of stars

> Deep into the darkness of her dreams
> dusk appears and smiles at me
> forever she'll be a daughter of the stars
> alive in the night with darkness in her heart

ELISE

Song of stars

Take care of your soul as you go
you mean more than you know

ELISE

Song of stars

She plays with the threads of destiny all around her
stirring the pot of fate louder and louder
come on let's live like thunder and wake up the stars
baby, sing your song and come as you are

ELISE

Song of stars

A flicker of flame in her midnight eyes
blink once for hearts
for a song, blink twice

ELISE

Song of stars

We move in the shadows and enter your dreams
mist in the night tells a forgotten story
awake in the lullaby of midnight's voice
you recognise yourself there and rejoice
once you hear the music of the stars
nothing can stop you singing with your heart

ELISE

Song of stars

She smiled with the secret meaning that we don't say out loud
and whispered
"it's all a game and some of us know we're playing."

ELISE

Song of stars

When the sun goes down
she wears the stars on her crown

ELISE

Song of stars

We ride with winter's wind on our wings
and on our breath are words we begin to sing

ELISE

Song of stars

When the wanderers of this world come home
and there's still wonder in their eyes
the wheel will turn again
and the stories will be shared

ELISE

Song of stars

> He could smell the desire in me
> like a wolf smells blood

ELISE

Inside her, endless
stories, songs and secrets

ELISE

Song of stars

I can hear parts of my song in your throat
and that's how I know
we'd composed it together, long ago
a way to find each other
in this musical play
in this theatre we call life

ELISE

Her day was for emptying inspiration onto paper from her soul
the night was for filling it back up again

ELISE

Song of stars

I recognised your magic for what it was
strange and eternal
makes me wonder about all the stories
that make my heart skip a beat

ELISE

Song of stars

I want to bottle your imagination
and drink in the night
to get drunk on your thoughts
and drift into dreams so
I can watch them come alive

ELISE

Song of stars

The artists of the world
the poets, writers, dancers, singers, painters, musicians
they know what it's like to pull from the hole inside
to create art from the essence of who they are
know that relentless feeling of tapping into the void
and filling it with their own creations

ELISE

Song of stars

You can't control my mind with your words
when I hear the beat, I'm in my own world
a never-ending pool of music in me
I hear my song, playing endlessly

ELISE

Song of stars

> My vitals are dropping
> my light is fading into itself
> then,
> I hear the stars
> my blood knows the music
> my soul knows the song
> baby, in these lyrics is where I belong

ELISE

Song of stars

There's music on the waves of life
for those with a signal
tune in

ELISE

Song of stars

Art is a representation of your soul,
so create what stirs inside

ELISE

Song of stars

> The beat of the electricity
> was pumping all our hearts
> flashing lights and her head went back
> and her eyes closed,
> and she breathed in
> the spark in the air
> and smiled because she knew
> this moment would burn forever in her mind

ELISE

Song of stars

Let's create sweet magic in this misery of maturity
let's be young, reckless and free
let's satiate the lust drive
and feel forever as we come alive

ELISE

Song of stars

> Haven't you heard
> you're what you've been waiting for

ELISE

Song of stars

> Turn on the sound in your mind
> leave all the empty noise behind
> just hear that ever-playing melody
> it's your song to sing

ELISE

Song of stars

It's no secret who you really are in those twilight hours
you're not afraid to bear your soul

ELISE

Song of stars

And we're all just wandering in the dark
dancing to the beat in our hearts
singing to the song of stars

ELISE

Song of stars

Orange and cinnamon mulled wine trickles down my throat
as I prepare my mind for the words I'm about to sing to you
in this sugar sprinkled fairyland

ELISE

Song of stars

Sunkissed flowers decorate my hair
as it twirls and billows to nature's song
with the taste of blood and nectar in my mouth
I whisper her stories I know so well

ELISE

Song of stars

As the sun kisses the Peruvian mountains
and her golden hair
shimmers with the silky light
silent echoes of people's songs can be heard
and the tales of stories whispered through time
come alive in the veil between day and night

ELISE

Song of stars

There's no need to read the lines on your hands
I can already see the destiny in your emerald eyes
and near you I can feel the stars caressing each breath you take,
you've faced yourself as deep as your mind goes
and made it all the way back to tell your story

ELISE

Song of stars

She travelled along the silk road to ancient lands
and crossed paths with strangers who would become friends
where everything began with the smile she wore
and the twinkle of adventure in her eyes

ELISE

Song of stars

She sat under her oak tree
and greeted the civil twilight ghosts
who came out of their shadows
to hear songs of glory and festivities

ELISE

Song of stars

She sent ripples in the starry waters
and gazed deep into the pictures she created
maybe her dreams
were the bridge between fantasy and reality

ELISE

Song of stars

Clouds snow cotton-candy onto her silver dress
and it's like the skies gifted her sweets
as she journeyed on further
into the mouth of darkness

ELISE

Song of stars

By her design she made her way through this world of songs
and painted exquisite art with her melody
she was the quintessence of story well lived

ELISE

Song of stars

So play the violin and hear the choir
only now, I'll fly higher
she said light the fire
the more fiercely it burns, the stronger your desire

ELISE

Song of stars

And wherever you are
the music of life
always mingles with
your heartstrings

ELISE

Song of stars

Cherry rum always washed down well
with sour truths you always came to tell

ELISE

Song of stars

If it was only a trick of the light
then why have I seen him before in my dreams

ELISE

Song of stars

A feast of figs, pomegranates and mulberries
with copper jugs of red wine laid on oak tables
illuminated by hanging candles
and adorned with lotus flowers
the hall was filled with laughter, honey
and the feeling of infinite wonder

ELISE

Song of stars

Fog fills the air
and footsteps are heard halfway to everywhere
maybe it's my shadow walking the way
I chose not to take
and perhaps we'll meet under falling stars
as the sky bleeds stories into our hearts

ELISE

Song of stars

> Never question the intensity of your desire
> if you can't sleep at night because of your raging fire

ELISE

Song of stars

You smell of freshly found love
and questionable morals

ELISE

Song of stars

Very quickly I learned to be
a dreamer awake and moving constantly
my desires also desire me
so whatever it takes, I'm all in, undoubtedly

ELISE

Song of stars

Don't be fooled by her beautiful
danger lies beneath
they call her beautiful poison
but her elixir wouldn't kill you
only show you the deepest parts of yourself
so you can look into the mirror between worlds
and face who you really are
like never before

ELISE

Song of stars

Oh darling,
when we jump into the unknown
we shake the magic within us

ELISE

'You're not like them'
she whispered, as she inhaled the fire's magic
'you haven't been broken by life'

ELISE

Song of stars

I was dancing with devotion
drinking down her potions
tell me, was it all you thought it would be?
did you dare feel the song of infinity?

ELISE

Song of stars

Caught up in a fantasy
maybe it was meant to be
all I know is what I feel inside
they told me to enjoy the ride
I lost myself for a moment there
caught up in the light of flares
send your signal fire loud
keep your mind wise and unbowed
girl, you're a diamond in the rough
the magic in you is more than enough

ELISE

Song of stars

Can you hear it calling out your name?
burning with the darkest flame
it's all or nothing in this game of shadows
you feel lost but you already know

ELISE

Song of stars

A string of thoughts in my head
dreams turn to nightmares in my bed
there's nowhere left to turn but to the woman inside
when all you've got is you, there's nowhere to hide
they say grow up with dignity
but they've forgotten the youths they used to be
don't let the fire die
baby, it's a lonely ride
but here we stand and here we fall
just get back up despite it all
look into that raging darkness
smile and blow a dreamer's kiss
because you are the only one who can sing your song
it's forever in you, beating on and on and on

ELISE

Song of stars

Under that eternal Mexican night
we didn't need your medication to get high
the music was ecstasy in our veins
the lyrics knew our names
that moment was yours and mine
let go of it all under those electric skies

ELISE

Song of stars

They promised us innocence, but it was all a lie
they promised us forever and told us to die
now I'll look them in the face
and walk with eternity's youthful gaze
it was never your choice what we could be
we choose to make our own destiny

ELISE

Song of stars

Taste of lavender pancakes
and maple syrup
in the soft light of spring
while we plotted ways
to heal the wounds we had made

ELISE

Song of stars

Playing with smoke and embers in her mind
starlight dancing in her eyes
so used to the agony of broken lights
but still, she smiles and shines tonight
it's never been an easy way
but that's how the gold is forged in the flames

ELISE

Song of stars

Maybe it was foolish to believe the world was theirs
when I've got a whole universe inside me

ELISE

Song of stars

Just let me know in the dead of night
if you can go all the way
I know by the look in your eyes
you're here to stay

ELISE

Song of stars

Mind so in tune with herself
she hears the answers to questions that haven't
even left her lips yet

ELISE

Song of stars

You didn't need to call my name
for me to know you were coming
I would recognise that body mist
of night's dew and truffle stars anywhere

ELISE

Song of stars

You've got that unquestionable nature of a girl
who knows her own mind
darling, show them how you fly

ELISE

Song of stars

Read to me in your secret voice
the one you keep only for yourself,
for me and for our midnight adventures

ELISE

Song of stars

I get lost in the music's mind
all else is far behind
who am I in that song
the lyrics are loud, and the beat is strong
dancing and dreaming with her melody
maybe I'm already all of who I'm going to be

ELISE

When the rules demand for you to alter who you are
break the rules, don't let them break you

ELISE

Song of stars

> We'll play the drums louder than they've ever heard
> we've got rebellion in our hearts, just say the word
> let them think we've fallen apart
> we're the ones that shine with the song of stars

ELISE

Song of stars

I kept a lyric book under my pillow
and dreamt of the poetry in your songs
baby where does your light come from
even in the dark, your music shines on

ELISE

Song of stars

My heart is bleeding the rivers dry
but I'll still kiss the dark in your mind
and we'll dance in the potential of infinity
for you, I'd show you all of me
and all the life I have inside
will flow like a river in my mind

ELISE

Song of stars

Follow me to the maze inside your mind
all the thoughts you set on fire
how many times will you go along with the design
before you recognise your own power

ELISE

Song of stars

Meet me where the shadows flicker in your light
bring your courage and your wits tonight
baby I can feel the song in you bursting to be set free
so let's take a walk into the nameless land for eternity

ELISE

Song of stars

But you've got a soul the electric lights run to
with that kind of lovely, I knew I'd find you

ELISE

Song of stars

So we'll risk it all tonight before the wheel turns
and if we fall or if we burn
we'll know we gave it everything we've got
no hesitation to pull the trigger with our one shot

ELISE

Song of stars

If you want a sad song, put your hands in the pot and choose one
but if you want a song of truth, be the one to sing it

ELISE

Song of stars

They all say 'there's something about you'
but I'm only interested in the ones who know what it is

ELISE

Song of stars

Tell me how I got so lost searching for treasure
maybe the gold has been inside me all along

ELISE

Song of stars

> I don't need your nightlight to guide me into the heart of darkness
> it's me at the door when the sun goes down
> give in to the desire drumming in you soul
> and I'll show you the beauty of the night and all her songs

ELISE

Song of stars

Sweet nothings may have got you this far
now I want to taste the sour in your heart

ELISE

Song of stars

Writing to get some clarity
I'm chasing the insanity
maybe these moments are made of something more than us
more than feelings of bliss
how can I describe this ecstasy in my heart
to someone who's never tasted the stars

ELISE

Song of stars

It's the look in your eyes before the beat drops
got me feeling like I never want to stop
let's ride this wave for as long as we can
promise me now and take my hand

ELISE

Song of stars

Like a butterfly's first flight out of the cocoon
to spread your wings is never too soon
listening to the thunder rolling over my fire
dreamers revel in the feeling of insatiable desire

ELISE

Song of stars

I'll fill my own cup honey
the time of dreamers is nigh
I'll plant thoughts with roots so deep
no one can stop that thundering beat

ELISE

Song of stars

I've never sang with someone
with as much life in their lungs
some songs can only be played
not in the studio and not on the stage
but from one heart to another
on a balcony in one world or another

ELISE

Song of stars

We found the splendour in nights that they'll never know
painting our hearts to put on a show
all the glitter in the world couldn't hide your true colours
so we'll sing this song or another

ELISE

Song of stars

She had the gleam of romance and passion in her eyes
an energy of dreams lived
and whispered fiercely
'just promise yourself, that you won't let the spark go out'

ELISE

Song of stars

The knowing in your eyes
had me breathing in desire
to peer inside your heart
and to show you mine

Song of stars

You didn't need to sing your song for me
I've heard it before
on the warm wind of the desert shores
and I remember every single word

ELISE

Song of stars

In her breath
I saw sparkles of gold
fly into the air
as we whispered stories
we'd never said out loud before
and would only ever say under candlelight
on that long, Parisian night

ELISE

Song of stars

> She had all the strength she needed
> but that night she let me see her vulnerable
> as we drank wine and starlight
> and danced to the harps of summer's orchestra

ELISE

Song of stars

Sound the songs to play tonight
no holding back the stars in your eyes
sing loud and true
with the voice inside of you

ELISE

Song of stars

Eyes hold the secrets to many wonders
and songs release the stories into the world
so when he sang
I got lost in the swirling storms of snow and smoke
in the darkness of his eyes
and felt the truth in every word

ELISE

Song of stars

She looked at him as if she could hear the song in his soul
and smiled playfully as she raised her golden cup
'to the stars who watch the meetings of like minds
and laugh as our stories unfold'

ELISE

Song of stars

And the poison makes me stronger
and the lies make me wiser
I'll fight for longer
on this highway, I'm the driver
you thought I was yours and you smiled
but baby, I'll always be mine

ELISE

Song of stars

She inhaled the sweet herbs
leaning against the stone balcony
and blew her thoughts into the night
a message to the stars
tonight, she would dance with her dreams

ELISE

Song of stars

> She's a storyteller
> who paints the stars
> with her soul-dipped words
> and lives by the lyrics
> in her starlight eyes

ELISE

Song of stars

Her sheer midnight blue dress
was made from the glistening sky
and that night she gazed upon her stars
and imagined all the stories they had to tell

ELISE

Song of stars

Lucid dreamers are out tonight
watch them dance with dreams in the sky
midnight leaps into the void and they fly
you know it's them, they've got stars in their eyes

ELISE

Song of stars

> I did what was expected of me for too long
> forgot to breathe, to just be young
> no more playing by your rules
> they never made sense to me, it's true
> watch me blaze the road I walk upon
> forget what's done, we're still young

ELISE

Song of stars

If I give up what I stand for
I may as well not be here anymore
so try and stop me if you dare
I'll play with the flowers in my hair
giving you the choice that you never gave me
and I'll win this game without a doubt, definitely

-Maybe it's not if you win or lose
maybe it's how you play the game

ELISE

Song of stars

Baby, your wings are showing
it's 3am where I'm going
don't be afraid of your light
you already know, I see it in your eyes

ELISE

Song of stars

Running out of juice in my soul
got to refill that subconscious pool
run away to seek my inspiration
that place of electric dreams and sweet imagination

ELISE

Song of stars

It's where my magic resides
in the darkness of your eyes

ELISE

Song of stars

> This is the realm of artist's souls, you'll find your way
> just be sure to paint what you really want to say

ELISE

Song of stars

Show me the sparkles of your soul
seeing that raw magic never gets old

ELISE

Song of stars

Windows down, driving into night's door
I can't be feeling this way anymore
open the lock on my mind
and I find all the answers are inside

ELISE

Song of stars

Mind never sleeps but wanders when we dream
all the world's beauty we have seen
call it energy of the soul or whatever you like
but something beautifully mysterious happens at night

ELISE

Song of stars

She carried the diamonds of her conscious mind
with her always
and you could see the glow
when she used that beautiful head of hers

ELISE

Song of stars

I put all my secrets in a song
just listen between the music

ELISE

Song of stars

'Can you hear it?'
'What?'
She smiled, raised her arms and tilted her head back
'The music of this world'

ELISE

Song of stars

And as we sat and talked of times long past
the flames sang our song of golden embers
and the smoke rose high into the night
carrying our stories onto the Northern wind

ELISE

Song of stars

But you know they want your soul
don't ever let them take you, you're the gold

ELISE

Song of stars

I poured the music of my soul into a song
and I wrote the lyrics where the light flickers on
I let my voice fly on the air that night
a story of stars shines so bright

ELISE

Song of stars

> Whistles, beats, tapping my feet
> the rhythm of life is yours to feel
> create your melody and write the words
> it's a beautiful song and you're the bird

ELISE

Song of stars

> Quarter to forever and I'm playing your song
> on my lips, where it belongs
> I got lost in the shadows of your mind
> dancing with your imagination, it's endless inside

ELISE

Song of stars

If they wanted us to be silent little girls
they shouldn't have put the instruments in our hands
and they wanted us to be perfect girls
but they must have known
we had our own songs to sing

ELISE

Song of stars

And the bard played his guitar
in the tavern under the stars
his stories came from near and far
and he sang of legends old
and thieves' gold
his poetry like a blazing fire on his silver tongue
all were drawn to his tales of courage and love
and all through the night his words kissed my heart
he gave me a musical feeling of hope on my travels through the dark
I'll never forget the glow in his eyes when he sang his song
like the stars that shine on and on

ELISE

Song of stars

All I need to tell a story
is wine, dopamine and a shattered heart

ELISE

Song of stars

Your poet's heart was bound to get broken in a moment
what matters now is how you get it to beat again, and keep beating

Song of stars

> The stories in my head keep me company
> when I'm high on life and no one's around to tell

ELISE

Song of stars

I only care about who you are in that moment
where it's all or nothing under the sparkling lights
when the music is flowing in your blood
and you can hear it in your ears like a daydream
come on, give me everything this night and every night

ELISE

Song of stars

Sitting with night's memory
you see yourself in the beauty
a reflection of what you see
in the waters of your destiny

ELISE

Song of stars

Smoking that passionflower in desire's lair
thinking of you and your hands in my hair
take me all the way back to that night in the city
being who we wanted to be was so pretty
you told me all your adventures that started with maybe
now we're here, singing all this poetry

ELISE

Song of stars

Let me play with the beautiful chaos beating in your heart

ELISE

The story of her song
is a tale the darkness knows all too well

ELISE

Let all the music pour from your soul and fill your cup

ELISE

Song of stars

I miss the sound of thunder in my heart
when you'd look deep into my eyes
and hear the hidden thoughts in my head

ELISE

Song of stars

She had a heart of mysteries and mayhem
oh, how I loved to let her lead me into the chaos

ELISE

Song of stars

I'm hungry for rebellious moments in the dark with you

ELISE

Song of stars

I could live off the high we get
when we run with the stars

ELISE

Slipping into weirder and stranger dreams
that seem to never end
and I can't pretend that it's not some victory
to dance with that eternal mystery

ELISE

Song of stars

> I just need some time to reconcile
> with the voice inside my head
> to be alone with my thoughts
> to dream until I'm me again

ELISE

Song of stars

You ever felt a story inside you
that rips your heart apart
and fills you with all voices from the void
that whisper moments from their lives
and stories from the times you were there too?

ELISE

Midnight music in my heart
and I'll stay awake
to hear the song of the stars

ELISE

Song of stars

Her golden voice sang the song of stars
and they smiled at her sweet melody
and while they toasted to a victorious night
she stayed under those stars
and drifted into a state of glistening euphoria

ELISE

Song of stars

Starlit dreams dance in my mind
under those desert skies
fire plays songs of embers while I sing
a story of nothing, and a story of everything

ELISE

She had the audacity of a woman who ruled the night
and she knew it

ELISE

Song of stars

My music sings
in my heart
and I can hear
the song of stars

ELISE

Song of stars

Thank you,

Elise

X

ELISE

Printed in Great Britain
by Amazon